● The City of Beijing

First published 2024 by
Redback Publishing
PO Box 357 Frenchs Forest NSW 2086
Australia

www.redbackpublishing.com
orders@redbackpublishing.com

© Redback Publishing 2024

ISBN 978-1-761400-72-8

All rights reserved. No part of this publication may be reproduced, stored in a retrieval system or transmitted in any form by any means (electronic, mechanical photocopying, recording or otherwise) without the prior written permission of the publisher.

Author: John Lesley
Editing: Caroline Thomas
Design: Redback Publishing

A catalogue record for this book is available from the National Library of Australia

Original illustrations © Redback Publishing 2024
Originated by Redback Publishing

Acknowledgements
Abbreviations: l—left, r—right, b—bottom, t—top, c—centre, m—middle. We would like to thank the following for permission to reproduce photographs: Images © shutterstock; pg6b cowardlion / Shutterstock.com, pg7b Nsbdgc, CC BY-SA 4.0 <https://creativecommons.org/licenses/by-sa/4.0>, via Wikimedia Commons, pg9tr Public domain, via Wikimedia Commons, pg11m Rolf_52 / Shutterstock.com, pg12tr Paul McKinnon / Shutterstock.com, pg12-13 maoyunping / Shutterstock.com, pg14tr Groverlynn, CC BY-SA 4.0 <https://creativecommons.org/licenses/by-sa/4.0>, via Wikimedia Commons, pg15br Chintung Lee / Shutterstock.com, pg16bl National Palace Museum, Public domain, via Wikimedia Commons, pg19 tangxn / Shutterstock.com, pg22tl Songquan Deng / Shutterstock.com, pg22bl ABCDstock / Shutterstock.com, pg23tr Gary Lee Todd, Ph.D., CC0, via Wikimedia Commons pg23br Shaun Robinson / Shutterstock.com, pg22-23m alarico / Shutterstock.com, pg24-25 testing / Shutterstock.com, pg30bl Bill Perry / Shutterstock.com, pg30m Map data ©2023 Google, pg32bl Eastimages / Shutterstock.com

Disclaimer
Every effort has been made to contact copyright holders of any material reproduced in this book. Any omissions will be rectified in subsequent printings if notice is given to the publisher.

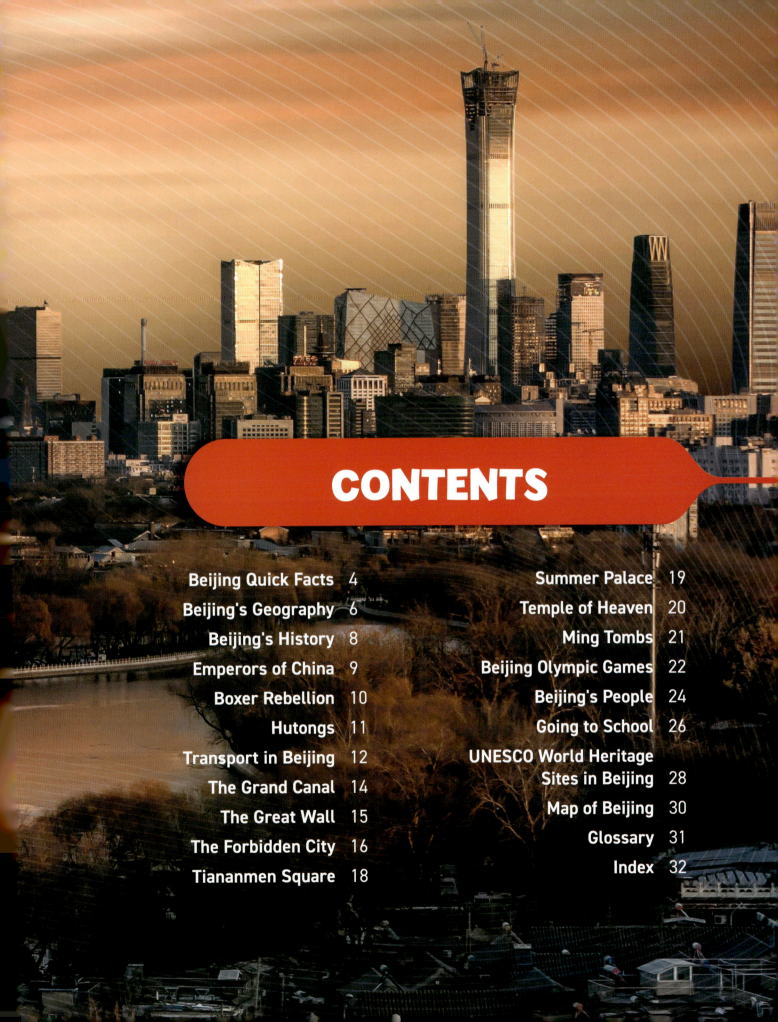

CONTENTS

Beijing Quick Facts 4	Summer Palace 19
Beijing's Geography 6	Temple of Heaven 20
Beijing's History 8	Ming Tombs 21
Emperors of China 9	Beijing Olympic Games 22
Boxer Rebellion 10	Beijing's People 24
Hutongs 11	Going to School 26
Transport in Beijing 12	UNESCO World Heritage Sites in Beijing 28
The Grand Canal 14	Map of Beijing 30
The Great Wall 15	Glossary 31
The Forbidden City 16	Index 32
Tiananmen Square 18	

BEIJING QUICK FACTS

Beijing is a centre of business, culture and tourism. It has recently experienced a dramatic rate of growth, driven by China's economic prosperity and rising living standards.

Beijing is the capital city of the People's Republic of China.

Beijing covers an area of nearly 17,000 square kilometres

The population of Beijing is over 21 million people.

● City of Beijing

北京

The Chinese characters for Beijing mean 'northern capital', because of the city's location in the north. In the past, the city of Nanjing, whose name means 'southern capital', was once the capital city of China.

BEIJING'S GEOGRAPHY

KAZAKHSTAN

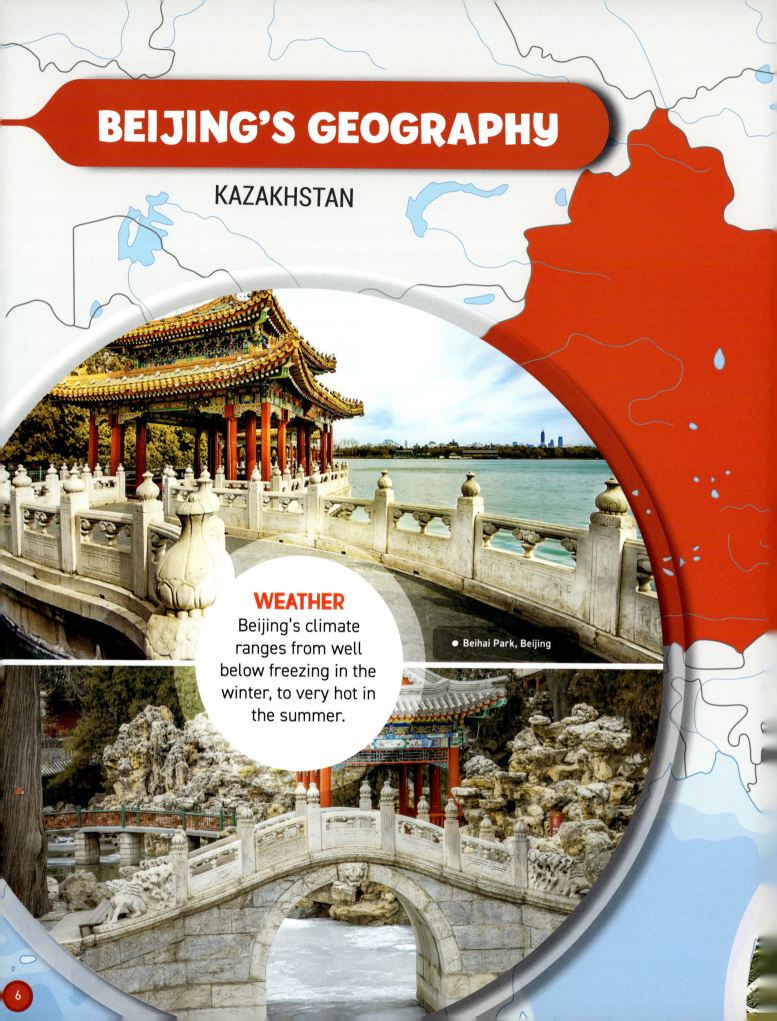

● Beihai Park, Beijing

WEATHER
Beijing's climate ranges from well below freezing in the winter, to very hot in the summer.

Beijing is located on the edge of the North China Plain, a large expanse of flat land that has an elevation of only 30 to 50 metres above sea level.

Beijing depends on groundwater for much of its water supply. Rivers that used to supply the city during its long history have recently experienced reduced flows, causing the Chinese government to undertake large-scale infrastructure projects to ensure the water supply for the future.

BEIJING'S HISTORY

Peking was a name that foreigners used to use for Beijing up until the mid 1900s.

The origins of Beijing as an important city go back 3,000 years.

THE STONE AGE

During the Stone Age, thousands of years ago, people were living in what is now the Beijing area. The discovery of the prehistoric remains of Peking Man in the 1920s made news around the world.

The Peking Man Site is now World Heritage Listed by UNESCO

EMPERORS OF CHINA

China was ruled by Emperors for 2,000 years. The last Emperor was only a young boy when he abdicated in 1911. He had lived a sheltered life in the Forbidden City, knowing little of the outside world.

● Pu Yi was the last Emperor of China

After the end of the Imperial Era, the Chinese people faced years of unrest, as various political groups sought to gain control of the government.

● The Forbidden city

The rise of the Communist People's Republic of China has resulted in a modern China whose ordinary people have lifestyles that are vastly different from those of their ancestors.

BOXER REBELLION

In 1900, the Empress Dowager Cixi and her officials supported a rebellion against foreign influences in China. The local forces, known as Boxers, tried to expel all foreigners, and fought against a combined foreign force. During the battles, large areas of Beijing were damaged, including parts of the Summer Palace.

● Ruins of the old Summer Palace

HUTONGS

In the past, Beijing had many hutongs. These are narrow streets which, together with houses, form neighbourhoods. Along the hutongs, people often lived in small, walled houses, where families shared central courtyards. Hutongs are disappearing from Beijing, but a few still exist to reveal to visitors the way Beijingers used to live.

TRANSPORT IN BEIJING

Beijing has all the modern transport options that its people need to get around, including trains, a subway, buses, cars, bicycles and taxis.

Beijing launched the first capital-city driverless cab service in 2023

The rickshaws that tourists love to travel in are an old-fashioned way of getting around Beijing, but they are not really an option used by locals.

BEIJING'S BULLET TRAINS

Beijing is a starting point for many long-distance train services operating across China. The high speed bullet trains are some of the fastest in the world, travelling at speeds of up to 350 kilometres per hour.

• High speed train, Beijing

THE GRAND CANAL

The Grand Canal

The Grand Canal is a man-made waterway built in the 600s to speed up the transport of grain from the south to Beijing. It was begun during the Sui Dynasty under the direction of Emperor Yang.

Over 1,000 years ago, Chinese engineers created the first canal lock. This invention allows boats to wait while huge gates close off the canal and fill an area with higher water. Boats can then continue travelling without getting grounded because the water is too shallow.

The Grand Canal

THE GREAT WALL

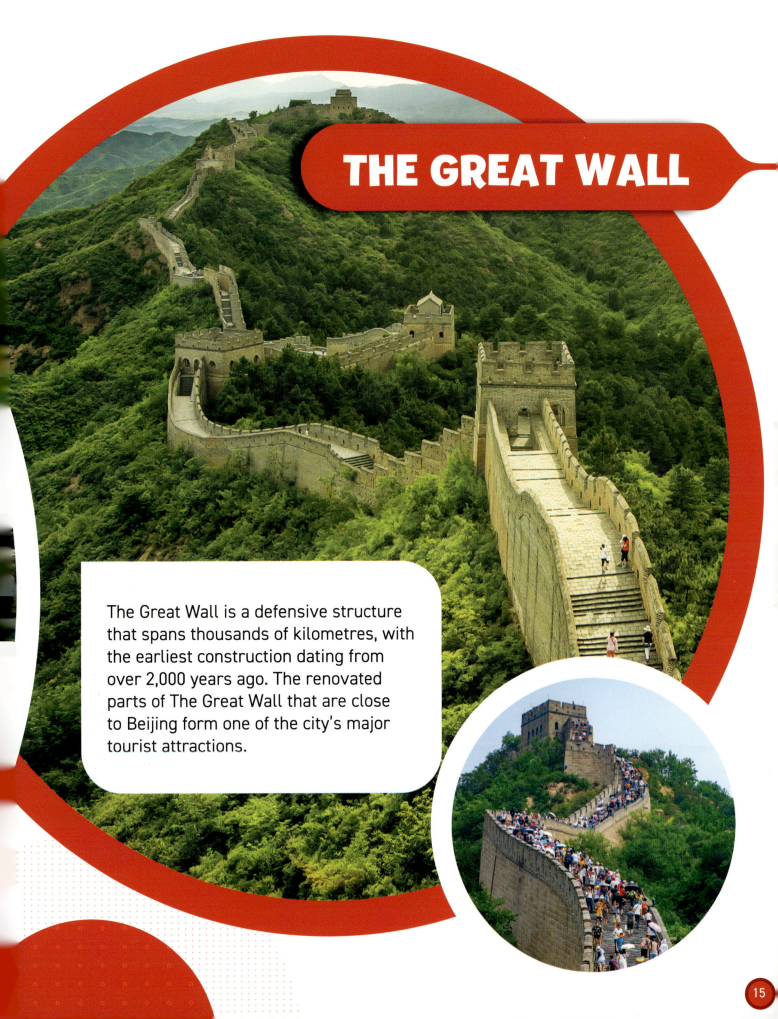

The Great Wall is a defensive structure that spans thousands of kilometres, with the earliest construction dating from over 2,000 years ago. The renovated parts of The Great Wall that are close to Beijing form one of the city's major tourist attractions.

THE FORBIDDEN CITY

At the heart of Beijing is the magnificent Forbidden City, dating from 600 years ago. It is the Imperial Palace of the Ming and Qing Dynasties and includes temples, palaces, residences and offices. The Forbidden City was once the centre of Chinese government and a home for 24 Emperors and their imperial families.

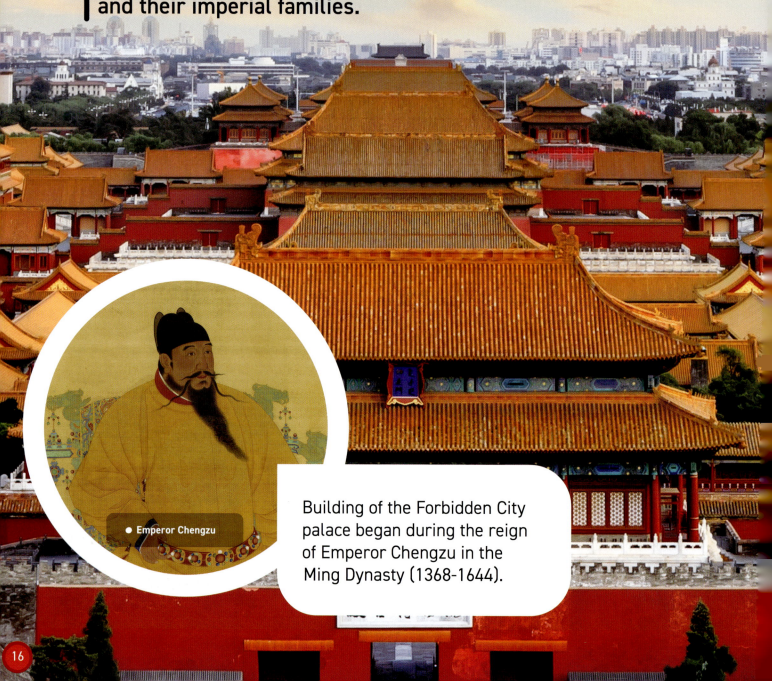

● Emperor Chengzu

Building of the Forbidden City palace began during the reign of Emperor Chengzu in the Ming Dynasty (1368-1644).

As well as the massive courtyards where public ceremonies were held, there are also many quiet, small spaces and gardens where the hundreds of residents lived and worked. A moat and high, red walls surround the Forbidden City.

UNESCO

The Forbidden City is a UNESCO World Heritage Site. It now houses the Palace Museum. Around 15 million people visit the Forbidden City every year.

TIANANMEN SQUARE

In front of the main entrance to the Forbidden City is a huge public square. Tiananmen means 'Gate of Heavenly Peace'. Thousands of tourists visit Tiananmen Square every day.

CHAIRMAN MAO
A large image of Chairman Mao Zedong looks down on the square from the Forbidden City walls. The Memorial Hall of Chairman Mao is located on one side of Tiananmen Square.

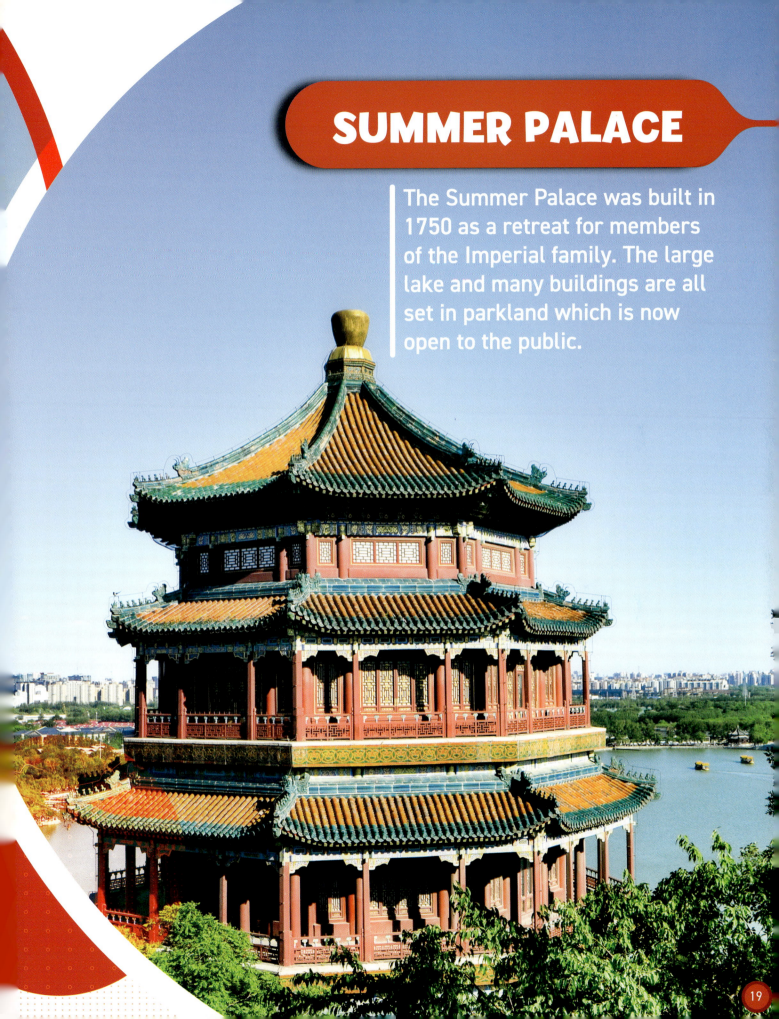

SUMMER PALACE

The Summer Palace was built in 1750 as a retreat for members of the Imperial family. The large lake and many buildings are all set in parkland which is now open to the public.

TEMPLE OF HEAVEN

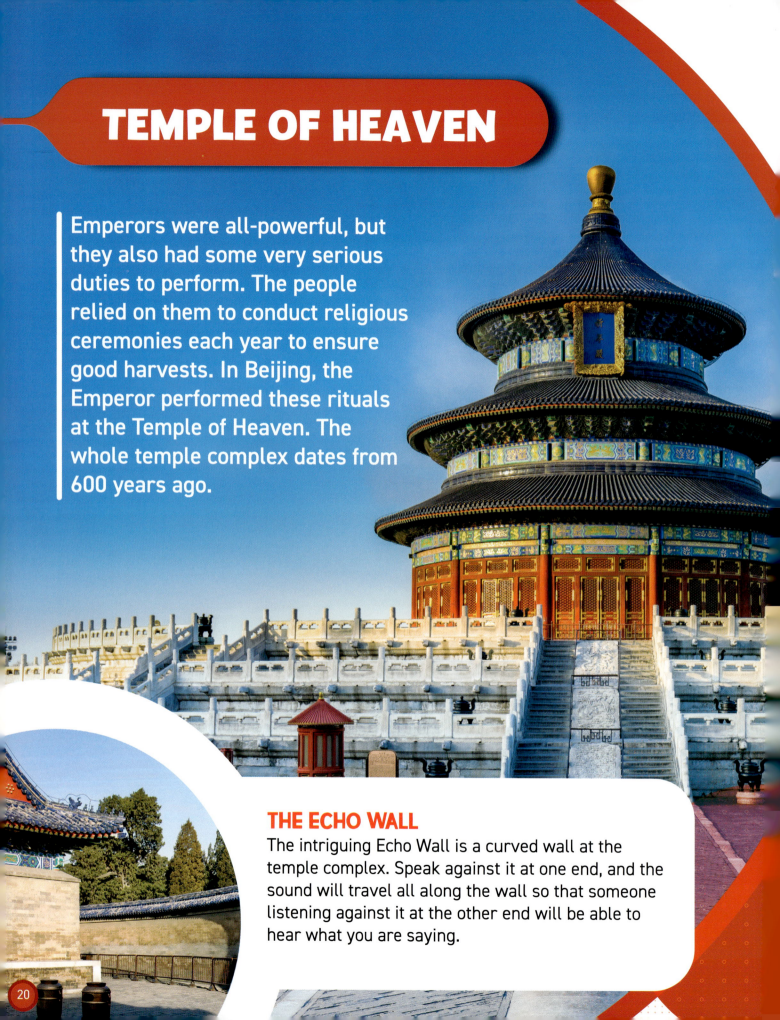

Emperors were all-powerful, but they also had some very serious duties to perform. The people relied on them to conduct religious ceremonies each year to ensure good harvests. In Beijing, the Emperor performed these rituals at the Temple of Heaven. The whole temple complex dates from 600 years ago.

THE ECHO WALL

The intriguing Echo Wall is a curved wall at the temple complex. Speak against it at one end, and the sound will travel all along the wall so that someone listening against it at the other end will be able to hear what you are saying.

MING TOMBS

The Ming Tombs and the Sacred Way are located just outside Beijing. They are the resting places of most of the Ming Emperors. China's Ming Dynasty lasted from the 1300s to the 1600s.

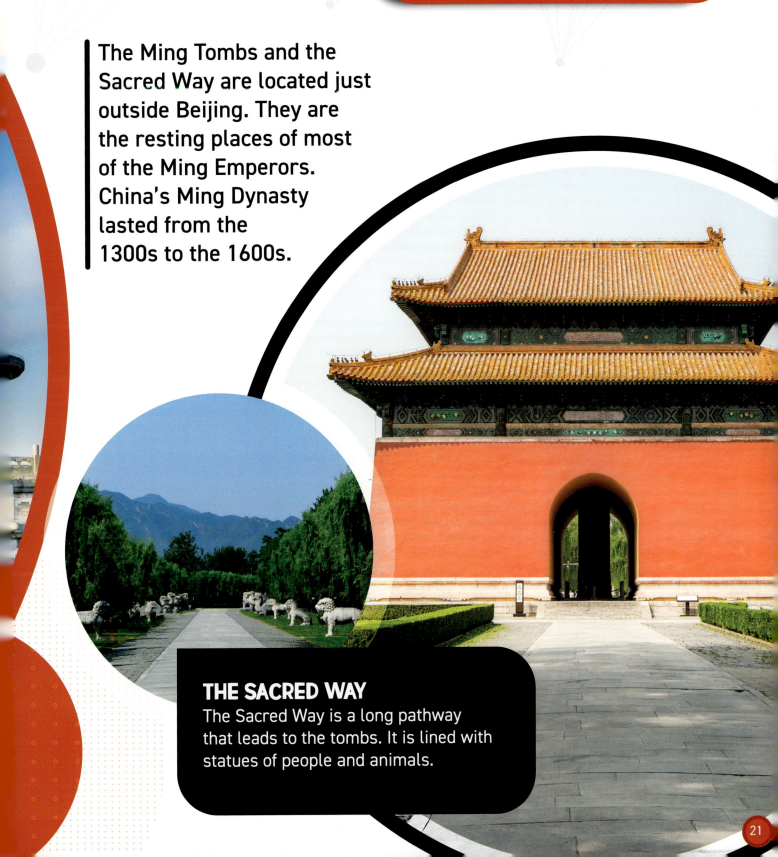

THE SACRED WAY
The Sacred Way is a long pathway that leads to the tombs. It is lined with statues of people and animals.

BEIJING OLYMPIC GAMES

Beijing hosted China's first Olympic Games in 2008, and built outstanding venues for the events.

BIRD'S NEST STADIUM
Beijing National Stadium is known as the Bird's Nest. It stands in the Olympic Green Village, which was in the Chaoyang District of Beijing City.

WATER CUBE
The National Aquatics Center is also known as the Water Cube. It was the venue for the swimming events at the 2008 Beijing Olympics.

THE TORCH
The Olympic torch that was carried in relays around the world was decorated with traditional symbols of clouds, which represent good fortune.

• The 2008 Summer Olympics Cauldron, Olympic Green Village

THE MASCOTS
The five Olympic mascots were Beibei, Jingjing, Huanhuan, Yingying and Nini. Read together as single words, these names translate as 'Welcome to Beijing'.

BEIJING'S PEOPLE

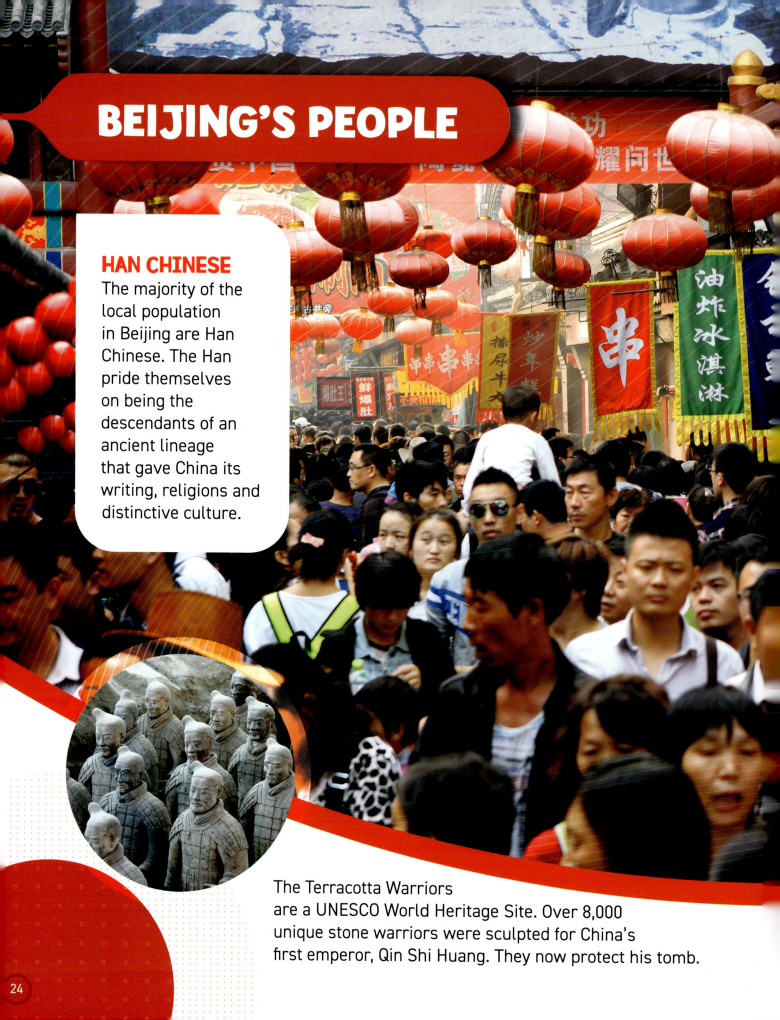

HAN CHINESE
The majority of the local population in Beijing are Han Chinese. The Han pride themselves on being the descendants of an ancient lineage that gave China its writing, religions and distinctive culture.

The Terracotta Warriors are a UNESCO World Heritage Site. Over 8,000 unique stone warriors were sculpted for China's first emperor, Qin Shi Huang. They now protect his tomb.

Beijing's population has grown at a very high rate in recent years.

Like the rest of China, Beijing used to have a 'One Child Policy'. This is no longer in operation, and families are now of many sizes.

Although Beijing is the capital, it is not the largest city in China. Shanghai has the largest population.

GOING TO SCHOOL

Beijing is a major centre for all levels of education.

Attending school is compulsory in China. Kindergartens, primary and secondary schools all have good teacher to student ratios.

• Guardian lions symbolise prosperity, success and guardianship.

A number of Beijing's universities, including Peking University and Tsinghua University, provide a high standard of tertiary education. Vocational and technical training is an important part of the education system.

Beijing is also a centre for International Schools that provide education for students from overseas.

UNESCO WORLD HERITAGE SITES IN BEIJING

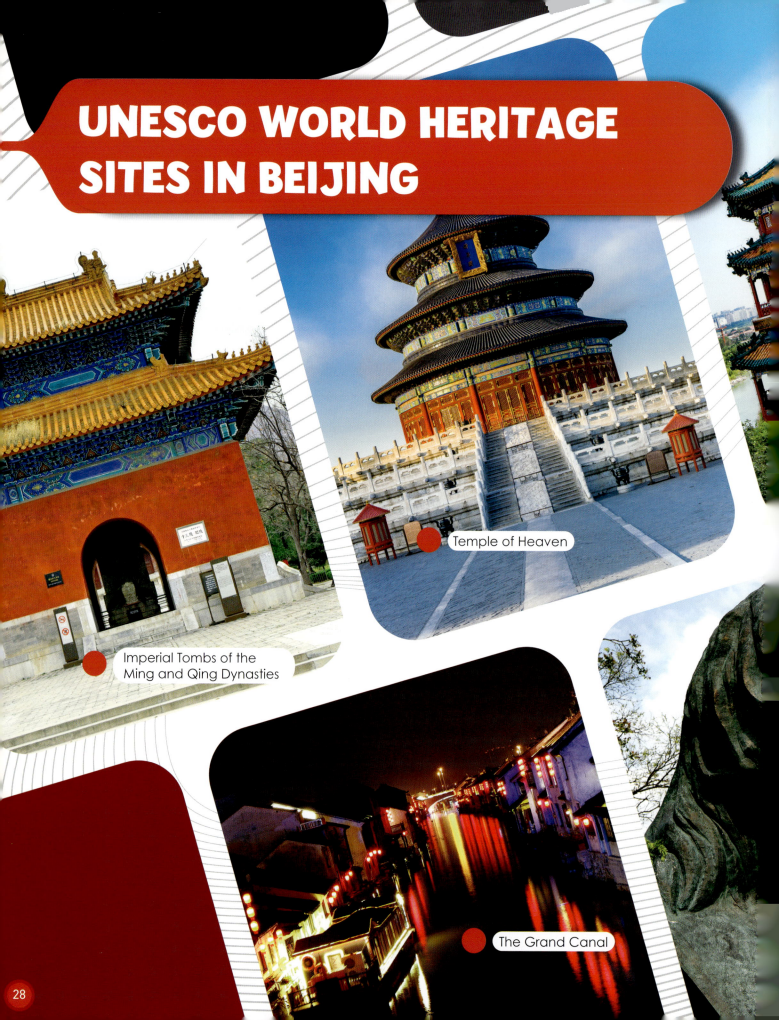

Temple of Heaven

Imperial Tombs of the Ming and Qing Dynasties

The Grand Canal

GLOSSARY

abdicate	step down from a position of power
elevation	height above sea level
groundwater	underground water source
infrastructure	construction necessary for a large project
moat	water-filled trench surrounding a structure
prosperity	wealth and success
ratio	number that compares two things against each other
rickshaw	two-wheeled vehicle pulled by a person
ritual	actions performed in a religious or other ceremony
vocational	regarding employment

The Great Wall

INDEX

Beijing City

Rickshaw

Bird's Nest Stadium	22
bullet train	13
Echo Wall	20
Empress and Emperors	9, 10, 14, 16, 20, 21, 24
Han people	24
Mao Zedong	18
Nanjing	5
North China Plain	7
Peking	8
Peking Man	8, 29
rickshaws	13
Sacred Way	21
Stone Age	8
Water Cube	22
water supply	7
weather	6